CHRISTOPHER
COLUMBUS

EXPLORER OF THE NEW WORLD

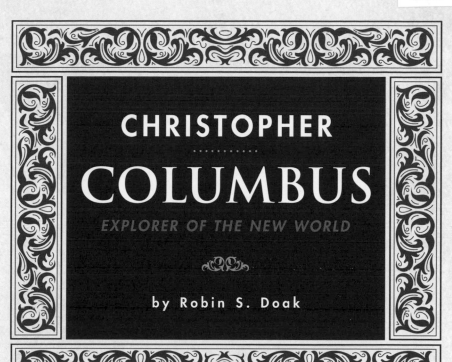

CHRISTOPHER
COLUMBUS
EXPLORER OF THE NEW WORLD

by Robin S. Doak

Content Adviser: William D. Phillips, Ph.D.,
Professor, Department of History,
University of Minnesota

Reading Adviser: Rosemary G. Palmer, Ph.D.,
Department of Literacy, College of Education,
Boise State University

COMPASS POINT BOOKS MINNEAPOLIS, MINNESOTA

Compass Point Books
3109 West 50th Street, #115
Minneapolis, MN 55410

Visit Compass Point Books on the Internet at *www.compasspointbooks.com*
or e-mail your request to *custserv@compasspointbooks.com.*

Editor: Jennifer VanVoorst
Lead Designer: Jaime Martens
Photo Researcher: Svetlana Zhurkina
Page Production: Heather Griffin, Bobbie Nuytten
Cartographer: XNR Productions, Inc.
Educational Consultant: Diane Smolinski

Managing Editor: Catherine Neitge
Art Director: Keith Griffin
Production Director: Keith McCormick
Creative Director: Terri Foley

Library of Congress Cataloging-in-Publication Data
Doak, Robin S. (Robin Santos), 1963-
  Christopher Columbus: explorer of the new world / by Robin S. Doak.
    p. cm. — (Signature lives)
  Includes bibliographical references and index.
  ISBN-13: 978-0-7565-0811-1 (hardcover)
  ISBN-10: 0-7565-0811-8 (hardcover)
  ISBN-13: 978-0-7565-1057-2 (paperback)
  ISBN-10: 0-7565-1057-0 (paperback)
  1. Columbus, Christopher—Juvenile literature. 2. Explorers—America—
Biography—Juvenile literature. 3. Explorers—Spain—Biography—
Juvenile literature. 4. America—Discovery and exploration—Spanish—
Juvenile literature. I. Title. II. Series.
  E111.D635 2004
  970.01'5'092—dc22   2004019029

Signature Lives

RENAISSANCE ERA

The Renaissance was a cultural movement that started in Italy in the early 1300s. The word *renaissance* comes from a Latin word meaning "rebirth," and during this time, Europe experienced a rebirth of interest and achievement in the arts, science, and global exploration. People reacted against the religion-centered culture of the Middle Ages to find greater value in the human world. By the time the Renaissance came to a close, around 1600, people had come to look at their world in a brand new way.

Table of Contents

1 A PATHWAY BETWEEN TWO WORLDS

⧌⧍

A shot rang out from the deck of the *Pinta*. Land had been sighted! After 36 days on the open ocean, Christopher Columbus and his crew would finally set foot on land—land no European had ever before seen. But it was two hours after midnight—too dark to go ashore. They would wait until dawn.

Columbus paced the deck of the *Santa María*, full of nervous excitement. He had sailed west from Spain and found land. Had he indeed reached the Indies? Columbus thought of what might lie beyond the small strip of beach—what riches he might be able to claim for Spain and what glory he might find for himself.

Columbus had begun his voyage seeking a westward passage to the Indies to make it easier to trade

After leaving Spain, Columbus and his crew sailed for more than a month before finding land.

When Columbus set sail on his first voyage, he was 41 years old—quite an old age in his time.

spices and other goods. He also sought to discover new lands and to find gold and other riches. He had pleaded, argued, and fought for years with the leaders of various countries for the backing needed to make the trip a reality. When he finally got the money and resources he needed, even those who provided it were still less than confident that Columbus could, in fact, achieve his dream. As time passed with Columbus still away, his doubters must have believed he had already failed.

Yet here he stood, just hours away from realizing his dream—just hours from proving himself to the world. As he stood on the deck of the *Santa María*, waiting for the sun to rise, Columbus must have felt that soon the world would be at his disposal. He probably believed he would soon be hailed as a hero by his crew. He certainly felt that his plan would be justified back in Spain, and that he would receive a royal welcome upon his return. He couldn't possibly have imagined the many journeys that still lay ahead for him, both on the open seas and in his own life.

As daylight broke, the voyagers went ashore. Columbus and his crew said a prayer of thanksgiving and claimed this new land for the king and queen of Spain. With banners and flags unfurled, they stepped onto land and into history.

Christopher Columbus is perhaps the most famous explorer of all time. His four voyages of discovery opened up a new and unknown world—the Americas—to the people of Europe. Columbus changed Europe's understanding of the size of the world. He was also the first European to see the islands of the Bahamas and the Caribbean as well as Central and South America.

Although hundreds of years later Columbus is remembered as one of the greatest explorers in history, he is also remembered for the many things that didn't go as planned, for the many failures that plagued him as he aged, and for his mistreatment of the native people he encountered.

Columbus's travels forever altered life in both Europe and the lands which came to be

Although many credit Columbus with being the first European to "discover" the Americas, the first nonnative people to explore the coast of North America were probably the Vikings, adventurers from Scandinavia. They left behind no permanent settlements, however, and had no permanent effect on the land and its people. The stories of Viking discoveries were not well known in Europe.

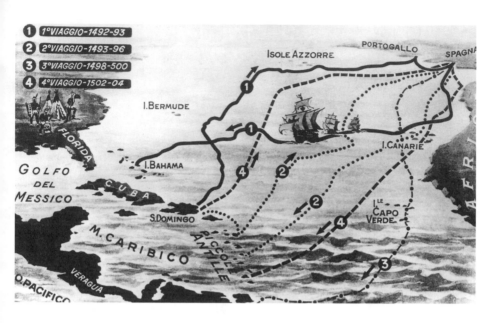

1 1°VIAGGIO-1492-93
2 2°VIAGGIO-1493-96
3 3°VIAGGIO-1498-500
4 4°VIAGGIO-1502-04

Over the course of his lifetime, Christopher Columbus made four journeys to the New World.

known as the New World. In the years after his voyages, plants, animals, and other items were shared between Europe and the Americas. People from Spain and other nations soon began colonizing the lands that Columbus had visited. For the native people in the Americas, the arrival of Columbus marked the end of their old ways and the beginning of many hardships.

Columbus himself never understood the true importance of his voyage. He believed that he had pioneered a new route to the Indies. But Columbus had charted a pathway between two completely different worlds, and in doing so, he opened up the New World to European exploration—and exploitation.

Columbus died without knowing how close he had come to discovering North America and finding all the wonders that were waiting there. He also died not knowing how he would be regarded around the world in the years to come. He couldn't have known of the many cities that would be named in his honor or of the credit he would receive throughout the world. He couldn't have known that the many explorers who came after him would use his experience as a starting point for establishing their own claims to greatness— that his discoveries would be the foundation for many, many more in the years to come. ✺

> *The Americas are named after a later Italian navigator named Amerigo Vespucci. In 1499, Vespucci began exploring the coast of South America. He was the first explorer to state that South America was a continent, not an island, as Columbus had believed. In 1507, a mapmaker honored the Italian's work by naming the continent America.*

2 A Sailor With a Plan

Despite Christopher Columbus's fame, many pieces of information about the explorer remain a mystery. For example, much of Columbus's early life is cloudy. Many historians believe that Christopher Columbus was born Cristoforo Colombo in Genoa, Italy, around the year 1451. At this time, Genoa was a major European shipping port.

Columbus's father, Domenico Columbo, was a wool weaver and businessman in Genoa. Later, the family moved to Savona, a coastal town near Genoa. Here, Domenico opened a tavern and sold wine. He and his wife, Susanna Fontanarossa, had five children. Christopher was the oldest. His younger brothers were named Bartholomew, Giovanni-Pellegrino, and Diego, and his younger sister was named Bianchinetta.

As a young man, Christopher Columbus studied charts and graphs to help him better understand the seas he sailed.

Genoa, Italy, was a busy port city in Columbus's time.

As a young man, Columbus was drawn to the ocean. It is believed that he first went to sea when he was about 14 years old. Although that seems like a young age, boys as young as 10 often went to sea for the first time as cabin boys. As he grew older, Columbus divided his time between helping his father and sailing the seas around Italy.

During these early years at sea, Columbus sailed

on voyages to Chios, an island off present-day Turkey, which was an outpost of Genoa during Columbus's time. He also sailed to England, Ireland, and Iceland.

According to legend, Columbus had a brush with death on one of his early sailing trips when his ship was attacked, supposedly by pirates:

> *[Columbus's] boat and a large Venetian boat were set on fire, and because they were locked together with grappling hooks and iron chains ... they could not be freed either one or the other ... and for terror of the fire, that in a short time grew so much that the remedy was for those who could to jump into the sea, in order to die that way rather than support the flames, and [Columbus] being a great swimmer ... taking an oar that he found, and helping himself at times with it, and at times swimming, it pleased God (who had saved him for a better thing) to give him strength to reach land, although so tired and exhausted from the wetness of the water that he took many days to recover.*

He came to shore on the Portuguese coast and quickly made his way to Lisbon, which he knew to be home to many Genoese. At the time, Lisbon, Portugal, was one of the most important trading ports in Europe. Here, Columbus was able to listen to the sea tales of sailors from other nations. He learned as much as he could about the ocean. He studied maps and charts of the known world. Columbus may even have worked for a while as a chart maker with his brother Bartholomew in Lisbon. And as a merchant, he made many voyages from Portugal, traveling along the coasts of Africa and Europe.

In the late 1400s, European merchants were becoming interested in finding a new route from Europe to the eastern lands known as the Indies. These lands included China, Japan, and India.

The overland route to the Indies was long and dangerous.

Europeans relied on spices to preserve and flavor their foods. These spices were brought from India by Muslim shippers and sold in Egypt to Italian merchants. These merchants charged high prices for their precious goods. If an explorer from Spain or Portugal could find a sea route to the Indies, these nations would no longer have to rely on Italy.

After years of collecting data and reading books by other explorers, Columbus began to make a plan for a voyage of his own. Columbus read Marco Polo's account of his trip to China, *Imago Mundi (The Image of the World)* by French Cardinal Pierre d'Ailly, and John Mandeville's *Travel Stories*. Columbus was probably inspired by these works, as well as stories of strange plants, boats, and even bodies with tan, flat faces that mariners claimed to have found floating in the ocean currents.

Columbus made a plan to reach the Indies in the East by sailing west from Europe. Like most other people in Europe, Columbus knew that the world was round. What he didn't know was the exact size of the world. In

The invention of the printing press gave Columbus and others of his time access to a wealth of information previously available only to the very wealthy. This machine, developed in 1454 by German publisher Johann Gutenberg, allowed for the mass production of books, pamphlets, and other printed materials. This important innovation helped spread knowledge and new ideas throughout Europe.

the mid-1400s, Europeans had a limited knowledge of the world. They knew about Europe, Africa, and Asia, but they had no knowledge of North and South America.

Many people laughed when they heard Columbus's wild ideas. They believed that such a journey was impossible. The distance to the Indies was too far, they believed, and the crew would run out of food and water. Columbus's mind was made up, however. He firmly believed he could find a western sea route to the Indies. All he needed was to convince someone to pay for the voyage.

By 1479, Christopher Columbus was 28 years old and ready to start a family. Around that time, he mar-

This illustration shows the lands Europeans knew of in 1492. North and South America are absent.

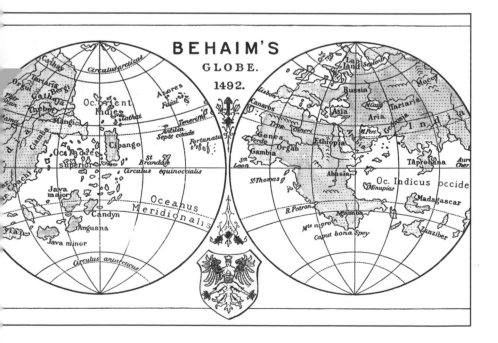

ried a young Portuguese noble-woman named Felipa Moniz. The couple lived in Portugal with Felipa's mother, the widow of a sea captain. Felipa's mother gave Columbus her husband's papers, charts, and maps.

Around 1480, a son, Diego, was born. Columbus's new family life, however, did not deter him from his planned voyage to the Indies. After Diego's birth, Columbus turned his attention to finding a sponsor to pay for his expedition. In 1484, Columbus presented his plan to King John II of Portugal. The following year, however, King John turned the would-be explorer down. John was already funding voyages to find a route to India around Africa.

No one knows for sure what Columbus looked like. Although there are many pictures of the adventurer, none were painted when he was alive. One of the few contemporary descriptions of Columbus comes from the explorer's son Fernando. He described Columbus as being of taller than average height, with light-colored eyes, a fair complexion, and blonde hair that had turned completely white by the time the explorer was 30 years old.

At this same time, Columbus suffered a personal tragedy with the death of his wife Felipa. Since there was no longer any reason to remain in Portugal, Columbus went to Spain to seek support, taking his young son with him. He probably entered Spain near the southwestern port of Palos, because he had relatives living nearby.

As a young sailor, Columbus visted ports throughout western Europe, and even as far as Iceland.

At some point between 1485 and 1491, Columbus befriended the Catholic friars of the monastery called La Rábida, near Palos. Columbus benefited greatly from his friendship with the friars. As he discussed his plans with them, several became great believers in his vision. Columbus spent many hours discussing geography with Brother Antonio de Marchena. Marchena may have played an important role in shaping Columbus's plans by pointing him in the direction of the ancient authors and church authorities whose writing offered support for the idea of a westward crossing of the ocean. In these same years, Columbus also met powerful noblemen of the region.

Among his supporters, however, probably no one was more important than Brother Juan Pérez, one of the guardians of La Rábida and a former official of Queen Isabella of Spain. Later, Pérez would intervene with the queen at the last minute, after Columbus had already been turned down once.

With the support of the friars of La Rábida, Columbus continued on to the court of the Spanish rulers. He hoped they might be willing to fund the expedition Portugal's King John had declined. ᕲ

Chapter
3 A SPONSOR EMERGES

❦

In Columbus's time, Portugal and Spain were great rivals. Each wanted to be the first to find a sea route to the Indies. Between 1420 and 1460, several expeditions funded by Prince Henry of Portugal, known as Henry the Navigator, sailed down the western coast of Africa in search of a sea route to India. None made it even as far as the southern tip of Africa. Now it was Spain's turn to enter the race, and Columbus had a new route to try.

Over the next six years, Columbus tried to convince the Spanish king and queen to fund his expedition. He talked to them about all the research he had done and showed them the map of the world that he had drawn himself. He enticed them with stories of spices, silks, and other riches waiting in

Christopher Columbus sought sponsorship of his voyage from King Ferdinand and Queen Isabella of Spain.

*King
Ferdinand
of Spain*

the Indies for the Spanish rulers to claim.

At first, Ferdinand and Isabella couldn't decide whether or not to fund Columbus's proposed voyages. They ordered a group of advisers, called the Talavera Commission, to examine Columbus's research and report back to them. The Talavera Commission was made up of astronomers, geographers, and other educated people. In the meantime, the rulers gave Columbus some money to help him make ends meet.

During the time Columbus was searching for a sponsor for his expedition, he met a woman named Beatrice Enriquez de Harana. In 1488, Beatrice gave birth to Columbus's second son, Fernando. Beatrice and Fernando lived in Córdoba, Spain, while Columbus continued to seek a sponsor for his planned expedition.

This was a very difficult period in Columbus's life. He struggled to make ends meet, living off the meager sums the king and queen provided for him. He followed the royal court throughout the country, and his ragged appearance and constant pleas for approval of his plan left many outsiders wondering whether he was even sane. His outrageous claims of incredible riches may have only made matters worse.

By mid-1491, Spain's Talavera Commission had studied Columbus's proposal, but the group was divided. Many decided that Columbus's plan was not very well thought out. Some members believed that the ocean was much larger than Columbus had stated. Other commission members, however, thought that Columbus should be allowed to try his voyage.

Queen Isabella of Spain

The Talavera Commission debated for months whether Columbus's claims could possibly be true. They argued about the wisdom of attempting such a fantastic voyage. Finally, after several more months of debate, the group issued its opinion: The expedition should not be sponsored. They agreed that Columbus's ambitious plan to cross the Atlantic to the west was impossible. Not only was the distance from east to west simply too great, but they also believed that the return trip against ocean currents would be even worse. Ferdinand and Isabella decided to listen to their advisers. They told Columbus they would not give him the funding he sought.

Columbus did not give up easily. He sent a letter to King John II of Portugal, asking him to reconsider the plan. Columbus's brother Bartholomew also tried to help, visiting the courts of England and France in search of a royal sponsor for the voyage.

In 1491, Columbus decided to journey to France to make his appeal to the French king in person. He left the Spanish court on foot, and headed for Palos, where he would would stop before continuing on to France. While in Palos, the dejected Columbus talked of his plans to Brother Juan Pérez, who had once worked for Queen Isabella. The friar himself traveled to the royal court to make a final plea for Columbus.

Spain had once been made up of many small kingdoms. In 1469, Ferdinand, king of Aragon, married Isabella, queen of Castile. Together, the two monarchs united the smaller kingdoms of Spain, creating one powerful Spanish empire.

Since coming to power, King Ferdinand and Queen Isabella had been engaged in an ongoing struggle to drive the Spanish Muslims, called Moors, out of Spanish territory. In January

1492, Spain won an important victory when they conquered Muslim forces in Granada, a city in southern Spain.

With the war against the Moors now at an end, the Spanish monarchs were more open to financing other ventures. Furthermore, for the first time in centuries, Spain was a unified country, ready to take its place as a world power. The Spanish rulers hoped Columbus's voyage would help make this a reality,

In 1492, Boabdil, the Moorish king, surrendered Granada to the Spanish.

and they agreed to support Columbus's expedition.

Columbus was no doubt pleased with the Spanish monarchy's change of heart, but he was also a proud man. His pride had been wounded by the constant refusals of the past and by the way he was perceived by the royalty and the common people of Spain. He had often been laughed at, and now that the king and queen wanted him, he decided to increase his demands for the payment he was to receive upon achieving his goal.

His pride, however, almost cost him the voyage he had long sought. When he made his new demands, the king and queen refused, saying the price was too high. Columbus left, riding away on the back of his mule. Fortunately, the queen quickly had a change of heart, and before Columbus could get too many miles away, a messenger found him.

Luis de Santangel, a key adviser to the king and queen, had convinced the royalty that they had little to lose in investing in Columbus's wild plan. The journey itself didn't need to cost much money, and the potential for great gains, should Columbus manage to succeed, made it well worth the risk.

Isabella and Ferdinand agreed to give Columbus a portion of the money he needed to make his voyage. They also promised him much, much more. The Spanish monarchs agreed that if Columbus was successful at finding a western sea route to the Indies, he would be given the title of Admiral of the Ocean Seas. He would also be named governor of any new lands he discovered and would be able to keep one-tenth of any riches he found.

In return, Columbus was commanded to claim all new lands for Spain. He was expected to deliver gold, silk, spices, and pearls to his sponsors. Finally, the Spanish rulers hoped that the explorer would bring Christianity to the people of the Indies.

In early May 1492, Columbus began preparing for his great expedition. With money from Spain, Columbus began looking for the ships, crews, and supplies he would need to complete his journey. One of Columbus's first expenses was to rent a ship, the *Gallega*, from a Spanish captain named Juan de la Cosa. Columbus hired the captain of the *Gallega* to serve as his first officer.

Columbus renamed Cosa's ship the *Santa María*. The *Santa María*, which would serve as Columbus's flagship, was a type of vessel known as a nao. A nao was a large ship that had four square sails and one triangular sail called a lateen. It

The Santa María, *was originally called* Gallega *because of its origin in a shipyard in Galicia, in north-western Spain. Columbus, however, considered the original name inadequate for a flagship of a Christian fleet, so he renamed it the* Santa María *after the Virgin Mary.*

also had a large forecastle, or raised deck, at the front of the ship.

Although no one knows exactly what the *Santa María* looked like, it is believed that the ship was between 75 and 98 feet (23 and 30 meters) in length, and about 25 feet (7.5 m) wide. Built to carry cargo, the ship was slow and difficult to navigate. Columbus later complained that the *Santa María* was "very sluggish and not fit for the work of exploration."

To repay a debt owed to the Spanish monarchs, the town of Palos was ordered to provide Columbus with two more ships. The *Niña* and the *Pinta* were both caravels—small, narrow vessels with three sets of triangular sails. Each ship could carry a crew of about 20 men, less than half the number the *Santa María* could carry. However, the two tiny caravels made up for their lack of space in speed and ease of maneuvering.

Now Columbus needed to find men and supplies for his voyage. To help their newest captain, the Spanish king and queen ordered that the towns around Palos provide Columbus with reasonably priced supplies. The monarchs also allowed criminals to delay their trials until after the journey if they signed on with Columbus, and several men from Palos did just that.

Nevertheless, Columbus had difficulty finding crew members for his voyage. Many men did not

Columbus's fleet was made up of two different kinds of ships: two caravels and a nao.

think Columbus's plan was possible and refused to sign up for the trip. Others didn't trust Columbus because he was an unknown navigator—and an Italian at that. Luckily, the captains of the *Pinta* and the *Niña* helped Columbus recruit crew members. Martín Alonso Pinzón and his brother Vicente Yañez Pinzón were both respected citizens of Palos. They convinced a number of men to go along on the journey.

By August 1492, approximately 90 men had signed

Martín Alonso Pinzón was the captain of the caravel Pinta.

on to sail with Columbus. Nearly all were Spanish. Three of the men on Columbus's expedition had come directly from the public jail. One man was a murderer, and the other two had helped him escape. The Spanish court offered the men reduced sentences if they would sign on for the journey.

The *Santa María* would carry the largest number of men—about 40 in all. In addition to the crew, a doctor, carpenter, cooper, goldsmith, and painter also traveled onboard Columbus's flagship. The *Niña* and the *Pinta* carried a crew of about 18 men each.

Shortly before sailing, Queen Isabella made Columbus's son Diego a page to her own son, Prince Juan. A page is a young man who serves a royal person. Columbus would not need to worry about Diego while at sea. And his companion Beatrice and younger son, Fernando, would remain safely at home in Córdoba. ✺

Columbus's son Fernando would follow in his half brother's footsteps and later serve as a page to Prince Juan of Spain as well.

4 SETTING SAIL

∽◌∾

On August 3, 1492, 41-year-old Christopher Columbus and his fleet of three small ships set sail from Palos, Spain. From Palos, they sailed to the Canary Islands, a Spanish territory off the west coast of Africa, to get supplies. Here, casks of food, wine, and water were loaded onto the three ships. Food supplies included hard biscuits, salted meats, nuts, dried beans, and cheese. On September 6, the ships headed out into the open ocean. The men onboard the three vessels would not see land again for more than a month.

Columbus himself had prepared a chart that he used to guide his way. In addition, like other mariners of his time, he may have used a compass and dead reckoning to help him find his way west. Dead reckoning is a system of navigation that

---

Columbus commanded his flagship, the Santa María.

Spain's King Ferdinand and Queen Isabella bid Columbus and his crew farewell.

enables a sailor to establish position and plot a course using direction, time, and speed.

During the voyage, Columbus kept a detailed journal for the king and queen of Spain. The journal was actually written in the form of dated letters addressed to Ferdinand and Isabella. Although the original journal was later lost, part of Columbus's account of his voyage was copied in the 1530s by a Spanish priest named Bartolomé de Las Casas. Thanks to the priest's copy, which included summaries as well as direct passages from the journal, people today have a fairly accurate record of Columbus's first voyage.

According to Columbus's log, the weather during the journey was calm and warm. When the winds would die and the ships would stop, crew members jumped into the ocean for a quick bath or caught a fish for dinner. Despite the fair weather, the crew began to get nervous and restless as the trip stretched from days into weeks. No one on board had ever sailed for so long without seeing land. Some began to whisper that the winds would blow them in one direction only, and never back to Spain. Some of the crew members even talked of mutiny:

As a young man, Bartolomé de Las Casas (1474–1566) watched his father and uncle sail off with explorer Christopher Columbus on his second voyage. Later, Las Casas himself would venture to the New World in search of adventure and wealth. As part of Spain's army in the Americas, he helped conquer and enslave the native peoples on the islands. Later, he would publish his recollections, along with his copy of Columbus's journal.

> *The more vain the mentioned signs [of land], the more their fear grew, they withdrew below decks, saying that [Columbus] wanted to be a great man at the cost of their lives. ... Those were not lacking who proposed they stop the*

discussions, and if he did not want to give up his plan, they could resolve matters by throwing him in the ocean, reporting later that [Columbus], while observing the stars, had fallen without wanting to, and that nobody would go around investigating the truth of it.

Many of the men traveling in Columbus's party were not well educated, and many of them were superstitious. They saw simple events and believed they were ominous signs of bad things to come. One night, a streak through the sky—perhaps a shooting star—made some men fear they were headed for danger. Others spotted seaweed in the water and thought it meant that trouble was coming. Many crew members also doubted that they would be able to find the proper winds to return home. They would gather in the holds below deck and grumble about the madman Columbus and the danger into which he was steering them. Some of them had a plan to turn against him.

At one point, a group of men approached Columbus on the *Santa María*, threatening mutiny if he did not turn the boats around and head back for Spain. But Columbus stood his ground. He reminded the men that if they did return to Spain, they likely would be put to death by King Ferdinand and Queen Isabella. The men weren't satisfied, but they must have realized at this point—30 days into the expedition—that their fates were tied to Columbus and his ability to find land.

According to Las Casas, Columbus decided to underestimate how far the ships had traveled in order to prevent his men from panicking at their distance from home. At the end of every day, the explorer shaved a number of miles off the total distance. Of the September 9 journal entry, for example, Las Casas wrote that Columbus "made 15 leagues that day and ... decided to report less than those actually traveled so in case the voyage were long the men would not be frightened and lose courage."

At the fleet's departure from Spain, King Ferdinand and Queen Isabella had promised a reward to the first man to sight land—a sizable yearly pension for life. Columbus kept the crew's spirits up by reminding them of the large cash prize that had been

The false distance legend arose because Columbus's journal bore two different sets of distance calculations. This led Las Casas to believe that Columbus had created a false log in order to prevent his crew members from realizing their true distance from Spain. However, there is another, more likely explanation for the seemingly false distances. Recent scholars have suggested that instead of creating a false log, Columbus perhaps first calculated the distance traveled using a method he had learned as a young mariner. He then would have translated that number into terms his crew would understand, creating a second distance record.

promised and encouraging them to look for land. He also told the men to think about the riches awaiting them in these new lands.

Despite his best efforts to keep his crew's spirits high, Columbus reported that by October 10, his men "had lost all patience, and complained of the length of the journey." The following day, however, the crew cheered up after finding branches floating in the water. Although they had already seen birds, crabs, and weeds, among other things, the branches were a sure sign that land must be nearby.

By the night of October 11, the signs of land had become more prominent. Columbus had lookouts posted at the front and in the crow's nest of each ship. He needn't have assigned the duty; most of the men were vying to be the lucky one who would spot land first and claim the royal pension.

Bermejo was later cheated out of his reward by Columbus himself, who claimed that he had spotted land before anyone else. As a result, Columbus was awarded the lifetime pension promised by Ferdinand and Isabella.

That night, most of the crew members on all ships stayed above deck. They stared to the west, looking excitedly for any sign of land. Finally, the moon rose, allowing some light to fall on the water. Two hours after midnight, on October 12, 1492 crew member Juan Rodriguez Bermejo from Triana, Spain, spotted land from the forward deck of the *Pinta*.

A cannon was fired from the *Pinta* to signal the other ships, and soon all the sailors were able to see the faint outline of land in the distance. Still miles away from shore, Columbus had the sails lowered so they could wait until daybreak to make their approach. He didn't want to risk having traveled all this way, only to have the trip end in disaster by striking some unseen hazard below the surface of the water. When daybreak finally came, the exhausted crew members prepared to approach the new land.

Columbus's crew was thankful to finally be in sight of land.

Chapter

5 A New World

⤶⧫⤷

No one is sure exactly where Columbus first landed. His descriptions of the island are vague and confusing. At first, Columbus described it as "small." Later, he wrote about the island as "good and big." All that is known for sure is that the native people living on the island called it Guanahani. Most historians believe that the first landfall was somewhere in the Bahamas.

Wherever he was on October 12, 1492, Columbus and his men stepped off their ships and into a new world. Columbus claimed the island for Spain and named it San Salvador. Here, he was greeted by the island's residents, members of the Taino group. Of this first meeting, Columbus later wrote, "I saw that they were very friendly to us."

After more than a month at sea, Columbus and his crew finally raised Spanish flags on the land they called San Salvador.

He described the Taino as "a loving people, and without greed, and docile in everything. ... I believe that in the world there are no better people or a better land, they love their neighbors as themselves."

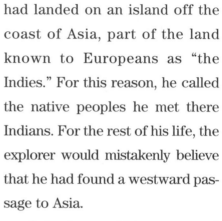

Some historians believe Columbus first landed on an island in the central Bahamas that was known as Watling Island. The island is a small one—only about 13 miles (21 kilometers) long and five miles (8 km) wide. In 1926, it was renamed San Salvador in honor of Columbus's voyage.

Columbus believed that he had landed on an island off the coast of Asia, part of the land known to Europeans as "the Indies." For this reason, he called the native peoples he met there Indians. For the rest of his life, the explorer would mistakenly believe that he had found a westward passage to Asia.

Columbus and his crew spent a few days unsuccessfully exploring San Salvador for riches. Finally, the explorer decided to set sail for China, which he thought must be close by. While sailing around the area, Columbus visited what is now Cuba and Hispaniola (present-day Dominican Republic and Haiti). He was disappointed to find no trace of the gold and spices that he had promised to Ferdinand and Isabella.

Columbus was impressed, however, with the beauty of the lands he visited. In his journal, he wrote about the region's great rivers, beautiful

mountains, green trees, and wide fields. In a letter to the king and queen, Columbus wrote,

On his first voyage, Columbus visited a number of islands in the region now known as the West Indies.

> [The islands] ... are so extremely fertile, that even if I were able to express it, it would not be a marvel were it to be disbelieved. The breezes [are] most temperate, the trees and fruits and grasses are extremely beautiful and very different from ours; the rivers and harbors are so

abundant and of such extreme excellence when compared to those of Christian lands that it is a marvel. All these islands are densely populated with the best people under the sun.

Columbus also wrote that in the future, he would provide

as much gold as you might need, a pepper spice, [to fill] as many boats as Your Highnesses might send to load ... and cotton ... and slaves. ... I believe I have found rhubarb and vanilla ... and when I return the people that I left there will have found another thousand things.

Unfortunately, the few spices that Columbus had found proved to have no commercial value.

The explorer became convinced that the area should be settled and farmed by the Spanish. As for the native people who already lived on the islands, Columbus believed that they could be easily converted to Christianity. He also planned to put them to work searching for the riches he was sure were hidden on the islands. In his journal, Columbus wrote that the Indians "are fit to be ordered about and made to work, plant, and do everything else that may be needed, and build towns and be taught our customs, and to go about clothed." Columbus also

Columbus hoped to convert the island's natives to Christianity.

wrote to King Ferdinand,

> As soon as I arrived in the Indies, in the
> first island which I found, I took by force
> some of them, in order that they might
> learn and give me information of that
> which there is in those parts, and so it
> was that they soon understood us, and we
> them, either by speech or signs, and they

have been very serviceable. I still take them with me, and they are always assured that I come from Heaven.

As fall turned to winter, Columbus started making plans to return to Spain. He collected plant, food, and animal samples to bring back to the king and queen. He also kidnapped a number of native people to bring home with him.

What Columbus still lacked was gold. In November 1492, Columbus ordered his ships to sea again, to search for new islands to the east where natives had indicated gold could be found. But Martín Alonso Pinzón, captain of the *Pinta*, headed off on his own with the speedy ship, leaving the sluggish *Santa María* behind. Columbus could do nothing but watch as Pinzón sailed off. Undaunted, the explorer continued through the open sea until he came to a new island. The new land reminded Columbus of Spain so much that he named it La Isla Española. It later became known as Hispaniola, and today is occupied by Haiti and the Dominican Republic.

Columbus had been warned that the natives of Hispaniola were cannibals, but his crew watched as the natives ran off to

The English word cannibal *comes from the Spanish name for a native group called the Caribs. The Caribs frequently waged war and, according to some accounts, would kill and eat any enemies they captured in battle.*

hide or brought gifts to the strange visitors. Immediately, the two groups were trading small items and communicating with each other. Columbus was careful to keep the ships far enough out to sea that they would not have to contend with the rocky underwater reefs as they navigated the shore of the island.

In the early morning hours of Christmas Day, while Columbus was asleep, the *Santa María* ran aground on a reef. Soon, the repeating swells of the currents were smashing and crashing the hull of the ship against the reef. Columbus tried everything he knew to keep the ship from being damaged further, but it was too late—the *Santa María* was finished.

Columbus's first order of business was to get himself and his crew off the doomed ship, into the ship's boats, and over to the *Niña* as quickly as possible. Once that was accomplished, Columbus faced a grim reality: His fleet of three ships was down to one, and a small one at that. There was simply no way the *Niña* alone could carry his entire crew back to Spain. Left with few choices, the explorer decided that the only solution was to establish a settlement on the island of Hispaniola and to convince some of his men to stay behind and operate it. Nearly 40 of Columbus's crew members would have to stay behind on the island.

Columbus faced another serious problem. The

Santa María still had valuable provisions on board—supplies that would be needed for both the voyage to Spain and for the settlement that would have to be built. But Columbus and his crew were not alone. A native chieftain and his people quickly came to help. Working alongside Columbus's crew, they were able to quickly retrieve the cargo and take it ashore. The natives also offered gifts and indicated that there were great stores of gold waiting to be found on their island.

Columbus soon began to believe that the wreck of the *Santa María* had been destined by God so that he would have to create a settlement on the island. He ordered his crew to quickly build a fort, using wood from the wreck of the *Santa María* and from trees on the island. Immediately, the crew began work, and volunteers stepped forward to remain behind in the settlement.

Columbus named the fort *La Navidad*, or Christmas, in honor of the holiday on which the *Santa María* was wrecked. While the fort was being built, crew members also were busy stocking the tiny *Niña* for the return trip to Spain, and Columbus readied himself for a triumphant return. The settlers were left with enough wood to build the entire fort, bread and wine to last a year, and plenty of seeds to use for growing new crops. Columbus ordered the men to collect gold and trade with the natives for

The fort La Navidad was built using timbers from the wreck of the Santa María.

anything else they needed.

In case there was any question about who was in control of the island after he left, Columbus gave the natives a final display of Spanish power by shooting the *Niña's* cannons at the damaged hull of the *Santa María*. On January 4, 1493, Columbus set sail for Spain, promising to return quickly to the first settlement he had created. ✍

Chapter

6 A TRIUMPHANT RETURN

In the beginning of January 1493, the *Niña* set sail for Spain. Columbus was worried. In his journal, he wrote, "[Pinzón] will be able to inform the sovereigns with lies so they will not order him to be given the punishment that he would deserve as someone who had done and was doing so much evil."

Shortly after leaving, Columbus and his crew spotted the *Pinta*, captained by Pinzón. Pinzón boarded the *Niña*, and Columbus confronted him angrily. Pinzón claimed that the winds had pulled the *Pinta* off course and away from the other two boats. Once they were separated, Pinzón claimed, he stayed on a nearby island to search for gold. Columbus was not satisfied with the explanation Pinzón offered, but for the sake of the return voyage

Columbus received a hero's welcome upon his return to Spain.

On the way back to Spain, Columbus recorded an unusual sight: "Three mermaids who came quite high out of the water but were not as pretty as they are depicted, for somehow in the face they look like men." Columbus was neither the first nor the last explorer to see "mermaids." These sea maidens were most likely manatees.

to Spain, he allowed Pinzón to continue as captain of the *Pinta*.

Columbus, however, was worried that he would not survive the return trip and that Pinzón would claim credit for his discoveries, so he wrote down an account of the voyage on a piece of parchment. He addressed the letter to Ferdinand and Isabella, wrapped it in waxed cloth, and placed it in a barrel, which he then threw into the sea.

Together, the *Niña* and the *Pinta* attempted the difficult crossing to Spain. The winter weather, however, made navigation much more difficult, and heavy storms tossed the ships. During one storm, the two ships were again separated, and Columbus's crew on the *Niña* began making vows to attend special Masses and made many promises to God to attend church if their ship could be spared. Finally, on the morning of February 15, land was spotted. It was the island of Santa María in the Azores.

Columbus sent a small crew of 10 men ashore. The island was controlled by Portugal, however, and the governor arrested the men, charging them with illegally trading in Portuguese territory. The governor did not believe their fantastic claims about the land they had discovered. Nevertheless, he eventually released the men, and Columbus was able to continue the journey back to Spain.

Again, terrible weather tossed the *Niña*. The sails were being torn to shreds, and Columbus's men were beginning to wonder if the world would ever know of their amazing discovery across the Atlantic Ocean. The journey back to the east lasted twice as long as the voyage west had. Finally, Columbus spotted land. It was land that was familiar to him, but unfortunately, it was not Spain.

Columbus landed in Lisbon, Portugal, on March 4. There, he met with Portugal's King John II, who was certainly not happy to hear of the success of the man he had turned away. By March 15, Columbus and the crew of the *Niña* made their way back to Palos, Spain. The *Pinta* arrived in Palos a few hours later. According to legend, when Pinzón and the crew of the *Pinta* arrived in Palos after Columbus and the *Niña*,

> *[t]he sight of the* Niña *already there, snugged down as if she had been at home a month, finished Martín Alonso Pinzón. Older than Columbus, ill from the hardships of the voyage … he could bear no more. He went directly to his country*

*house near Palos, took to his bed, and died
within a month.*

In Palos, Columbus received a hero's welcome
and was honored with feasts and parties. When he
appeared before Ferdinand and Isabella in Seville, he
offered them corn, potatoes, tobacco, parrots, and
the seven natives he had captured. He also presented
a few small samples of gold and pearls.

While presenting these gifts to the king and
queen, Columbus greatly exaggerated the value of
what he had found. After his first voyage, he promised the king and queen,

> *in seven years from today I will be able to
> pay Your Highnesses for five thousand
> cavalry and five thousand foot soldiers.
> … And all of this with very little invest-
> ment now on Your Highnesses' part in
> this beginning of the taking of the Indies
> and all that they contain.*

Although Columbus claimed to have found the
Indies, not everyone believed him. Soon after the
explorer returned from his voyage, a Spanish
courtier wrote a letter discussing Columbus:

> *A certain Colón navigated towards the
> West until reaching the coasts of the*

Although Columbus showed the Spanish king and queen samples of the island's riches, he promised more than he was able to deliver.

Indies—as he believes. … He found many islands and it is believed that they are the ones mentioned farther away … and adjacent to India. I do not deny it completely, although the magnitude of the world seems to indicate the opposite.

The courtier was correct—Columbus had not sailed all the way to the Indies, nor had he found the vast riches he claimed or promised. Yet the king and queen were thrilled with Columbus's discoveries. They paid great honor to Columbus, allowing him to sit in their presence with his hat on and ride on horseback next to the king. He was also awarded tht title he had been promised—Admiral of the Ocean Seas—as well as that of Viceroy and Governor of the Indies.

In addition to his new titles, the Spanish king and queen honored Columbus with a book of privileges and a coat of arms.

Most importantly, Ferdinand and Isabella decided to pay for a second voyage. Columbus assured the monarchs that on his next trip, he would bring them

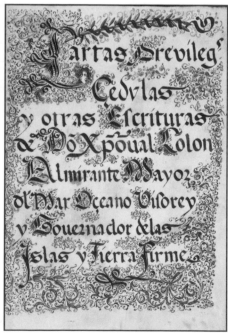

the gold, spices, and silk in "Asia" that he knew were there. Columbus also promised to set up Spanish colonies in the new lands he had found.

Shortly after Columbus arrived home, King John II tried to claim the newly found land for Portugal. He based his claims on the voyages of the Portuguese explorers who had been looking for routes to the Indies by way of Africa. To protect their interests in the New World, King Ferdinand and Queen Isabella sent ambassadors to the pope, the head of the Roman Catholic Church. As head of the Roman Catholic Church and God's representative on Earth, the pope claimed the right to rule over all Catholic monarchs. The Spanish ambassadors told the pope of the discoveries Columbus had made for Spain. They requested and received a decree from the pope that gave Spain control of these new lands. But Portugal refused to accept the decree. At Columbus's suggestion, the rulers of the two countries met to settle the matter. They drew a line on a map down the 46th meridian. All discoveries east of the line would belong to Portugal, and all discoveries west of the line would belong to Spain—no matter which country made the discovery. ℘

Chapter

7 BACK TO THE NEW WORLD

ecᕮᕮᕬᕬᕫᕫᕫᕫᕫᕫᕫᕫᕫ

On September 25, 1493, Columbus set sail from Cádiz, Spain, on his second voyage of discovery. This time, the explorer departed in grand style. He had a fleet of 17 ships carrying livestock for the New World. Among them was a ship from the first voyage—the caravel *Niña*. It had been renamed *Santa Clara* for the new trip.

Along for the ride were about 20 experienced farmers, tradesmen, and artisans. As many as 1,500 men joined the expedition, hoping to become wealthy from the riches of the Indies and establish a Spanish settlement in the area.

Before he left, Columbus received a number of orders from Ferdinand and Isabella. One order charged him to "try and work to bring the residents

Back in the New World, Columbus sought the natives' help in finding greater riches.

of said islands and mainland to convert to our Holy Catholic faith." The king and queen also laid out the form of government they wanted in their new lands, with Columbus in charge as the governor. For the time being, Columbus was given the power to appoint officials to help him run the islands he had found.

One important order concerned how the Spanish were expected to treat the island natives. The order read, "The Indians [must] be well treated and any who offends them be severely punished." A Catholic priest, Father Buil, was sent with Columbus to ensure that this order was followed. The priest was to report directly to the king and queen.

Columbus's second voyage was plagued with problems from the very start. Poorly constructed barrels caused meat and other food supplies to spoil. Water supplies ran low. After an uncomfortable month at sea, the fleet arrived at what are now known as the Leeward Islands in the West Indies.

Columbus's first stop was an island he named Dominica. On the nearby island that is now known as Guadeloupe, Columbus

If Columbus kept a journal during his second trip to the New World, it has unfortunately been lost. The information about this journey has come down through the years from other sources. These sources include letters written by Columbus, as well as the accounts of others who were on the voyages or had information about them.

The king and queen sent Father Buil, a priest, to make sure Columbus treated the natives fairly.

first made contact with the Carib people. The Caribs were a group of native tribes whom Columbus believed to be cannibals. The Carib men fled into the forests when he arrived, but Columbus captured several women and a young boy. Before leaving the island, Columbus burned the natives' canoes, but not their homes. "I did not burn their houses so that we could use them when we pass by here, because it is on the route to Spain," Columbus wrote later.

When Columbus finally reached Hispaniola, he met with an awful surprise. All of the men he had left behind at La Navidad were dead. The little fort, built mainly with the wood of the *Santa María*, had been destroyed. Columbus later learned that the crew had treated the natives cruelly. Although nobody really knows how the Spaniards at La Navidad died, some suspect that the natives had responded to their brutal treatment by killing many of the Spaniards. Some of the men may have been killed by disease, while others might have died fighting one another.

In early January 1494, Columbus and his men ventured into the interior of Hispaniola and began building a new settlement. Columbus named his new town Isabela after the queen of Spain. In a letter to the king and queen, he described the site in glowing terms:

> *Storms never enter here ... which is marvelous land without comparison to any in [Spain] ... there is tall and green grass everywhere and much better than barley in Spain in the best time.*

The new settlers set to work building huts for themselves out of straw and palm leaves. Public buildings, like the church, were made out of stone. However, the settlement was a small one, with little space available for those who had journeyed from Spain. According to one historian, each man in Columbus's party probably had about 12 square feet (1 square meter) of living space.

Bad luck plagued the expedition. Many of the Spanish settlers—including Columbus—became seriously ill after arriving. Some historians believe that the illnesses might have been the result of unclean living arrangements or lack of food. By

April 1494, only about 800 of the roughly 1,500 original settlers remained alive. Columbus wrote,

This rocky beach marks the site where the settlement of Isabela once stood.

> *One night I left the village ... to see a port ... and, at the time I went to sleep my right side tormented me, from the bottom of the foot up to my head, as with palsy, from which I have suffered not little pain.*

After establishing the town of Isabela, Columbus and his men explored Hispaniola and the surrounding islands. Columbus was anxious to find the gold and spices he had promised the rulers of Spain. On this expedition, he visited present-day Jamaica, Dominica, Guadeloupe, and Puerto Rico. Columbus mistakenly believed they were islands off the coast of Japan. He also visited Cuba, which he believed to be the mainland of China. He was so convinced of this that he made his men sign a statement that said they agreed with him. Anyone who refused to sign was threatened with a heavy fine and to "have his tongue cut out."

While Columbus was exploring, he left his brother Diego and Father Buil in charge of the town of Isabela. Later, Columbus's brother Bartholomew arrived from Spain with much-needed supplies, and he, in turn, took control of the new Spanish colony.

While he may have been a good mariner, Columbus was a poor governor. Natives and Spanish settlers alike found him harsh and severe. The natives were abused by many members of the expedition. The Spanish stole the natives' food, wives, and daughters. The natives believed that Columbus and the Spanish were "intolerable, fierce, cruel, and knew no reason."

Columbus wrote about how he and his men treated natives who defied the Spanish. In one letter, he described the punishment that awaited a pair of natives who had stolen a sword and some clothing from his soldiers: "And the boy of the sword and the other, he took in the middle of the plaza, in front of everybody … tied them there and cut off their ears."

Even some Spaniards found it difficult to be governed by Columbus. When building the colony of Isabela, Columbus made all of his men pitch in, including those who were unused to manual labor. Those who refused to help were severely punished.

Soon, some men began to defy Columbus. Father Buil, the priest sent to keep an eye on him, may have been one such man. According to one story, Father Buil became angry with Columbus when the explorer ordered a Spaniard to be hanged. He showed his anger by refusing to hold church services. In return, Columbus refused food to the priest and his men.

Columbus ordered one of his own men to be publicly hanged, angering the priest, Father Buil.

In September 1494, Father Buil and a group of men set sail for Spain. While some, including the priest, were ill, others may have decided that life in the New World was not what they expected. They were the first of many to give up on the new colony.

Spaniards and natives alike were suffering from hunger, as well. The two groups competed against one another for the limited supplies of food on the island, and the Spaniards won. At one point, the native Tainos stopped planting crops in the hopes

An early woodcut of the area visited by Columbus

that the Spaniards would leave them alone, but their plan backfired. The natives were forced to rely on roots for food, and they began to die of starvation. Columbus wrote, "Hunger has been the cause of the death of more than two thirds of them, and it is not over nor is it known when the end can be expected."

The dying out of the native Taino people, resulting from both hunger and disease, would have consequences that would reach as far as Africa. In the coming years, Columbus and other Spanish governors would bring in African slaves to work in their mines and on their plantations. This was the beginning of a system of slavery that would persist in the New World for more than 300 years.

By early 1496, Columbus was ready to return to Spain. First, however, he would have to find a way to get back home. Foul weather had taken a serious toll on his fleet, and most of his ships had been damaged or destroyed. Columbus solved his transportation problems by using the wrecks of some ships to repair a damaged boat and to build a new one.

On March 10, 1496, Columbus set sail for Spain, leaving his brothers Bartholomew and Diego in control of the colony he had founded. His two ships limped into the Spanish port of Cádiz in July, about four months after they had set sail. For the second time, Columbus had returned without the riches that he had promised. ✒

8 THE THIRD VOYAGE

Chapter

❧❧❧

Columbus was not yet ready to give up on finding the wealth he had promised Spain. Although they considered his first two expeditions to be financial failures, Ferdinand and Isabella nevertheless agreed to allow him to try again. This time, however, Columbus's mission would be to bring supplies to the new colony. And he would command a scaled-back fleet of only six ships.

By now, people throughout Spain had heard about the struggling colony. Few, however, were anxious to move there. So, to encourage settlement, the Spanish monarchs offered to pardon any criminals who would agree to go on Columbus's third expedition. Ten murderers took advantage of the deal and signed up. Still, Columbus was unable to fill his ships.

The third voyage did not end well for Columbus.

In a letter to Ferdinand and Isabella, written during the third voyage, Columbus discussed his theory that the world was not, in fact, round: "I find that [the world] is not round as they describe it, but that it is the shape of a pear which is everywhere round except where the stalk is." Columbus went on to describe a part of the world that rose high into the sky, which he named the "end of the East." He believed that a paradise on Earth could be found there.

On May 30, 1498, Columbus set out on his third expedition. Despite his orders to deliver supplies to Hispaniola, the explorer had a different plan. He sent three ships to the Spanish colony, but took the remaining three ships to explore the region. On this voyage, Columbus visited present-day Trinidad, Tobago, Grenada, and Margarita. He also caught a glimpse of the coast of South America, most likely Venezuela. Columbus, however, believed that he was seeing another island.

Off the coast of Venezuela, Columbus and his men made one of his most important and valuable finds: pearls. Columbus sent a shipment of the precious gems back to Spain. Before long, pearl traders were setting sail for the Pearl Coast, as the area came to be known. The find also greatly encouraged the king and queen of Spain. Until now, little of value had been brought back from the New World.

On the Pearl Coast, Columbus encountered a native people unlike any he had previously met. Their culture was much more developed than any of

the others, and they had developed the ability to make their own jewelry, much of it from gold. They quickly traded with these natives, who were equally eager to obtain items from a foreign land.

Venezuela's Pearl Coast promised new riches for Columbus and the Spanish court.

When Columbus finally arrived in Hispaniola on August 31, 1498, trouble was waiting. His brothers had proven to be as poor at governing as Columbus himself. A new capital, Santo Domingo, had been founded on the island, and settlers there were having the same problems as the settlers in Isabela. Little food was left on the island, and about half of the Spaniards were on the point of rebellion. Many of the native Tainos who had been forced to pan for gold and work in the fields had either died from disease or fled.

Columbus tried to restore order by hanging some of the rebels. However, he was unable to fix the problems in Hispaniola. By 1499, the king and queen had gotten word that things were falling apart in the New World. In August 1500, a new governor, Francisco de Bobadilla, arrived from Spain. Not long after coming ashore, he saw signs of trouble. Seven natives hung from trees, and five more were to be hanged later that day. Soon, those Spaniards who were against Columbus and his brothers came forward with other terrible stories. Bobadilla arrested Columbus and his two brothers, put them in chains, and sent them home to Spain where they would stand trial.

Columbus's brother Bartholomew was as poor a governor as Columbus himself.

The trip back to Spain was humiliating for the proud explorer. According to his son Fernando, Columbus chose to always remember his imprisonment at the hands of the king and queen of Spain. For the rest of his life, the explorer kept in his bedroom the chains that he wore on the voyage from Hispaniola. Fernando also wrote that his father had requested to be buried with the chains in his casket.

Diego Columbus, along with Columbus and his brother Bartholomew, was sent back to Spain in chains.

Nevertheless, when Columbus arrived in Spain, he was able to convince Ferdinand and Isabella of his innocence. The king and queen released him and restored his titles of admiral and viceroy. They made it clear to him, however, that the titles were now empty ones. Columbus was to have no authority or power in the New World colonies.

Columbus's habit of exaggeration continued throughout his lifetime. Even after finding few goods of value on his third voyage, Columbus told the king and queen that "the door to the gold and pearls is now open, and all in great quantity, precious

Columbus managed to convince the queen of his innocence.

stones and spices and a thousand things can be expected with confidence."

For the past three voyages, Columbus had

promised King Ferdinand and Queen Isabella that he would shower them with great riches upon his next return, and each time he had returned with only more promises. But although their patience was wearing thin, the Spanish monarchs agreed to allow Columbus to make a fourth trip to the New World. They told Columbus, however, that he would no longer be welcome on the island of Hispaniola. They also refused to give him any money for his voyage. Although the king and queen granted his request for ships, Columbus would have to gather the needed funds for the journey he called his "high voyage" on his own. ❧

9 THE FINAL VOYAGE

Chapter

ᴄ∞ᴏ

Columbus's fourth voyage began on May 9, 1502. This time, he commanded four ships and about 150 men. One of the crew members was Columbus's 13-year-old son Fernando, the child of Columbus and his companion, Beatrice Enriquez de Harana. Columbus had a close relationship with his teen-aged son. In 1504, he would write about Fernando to his oldest son Diego, "Although [Fernando] is a child by age, he is not so in understanding."

Columbus saw this voyage as a way to restore his honor and good name in the eyes of the world. This time, he was determined to find the western passage to India. He was so convinced that he would reach India and China that he brought a letter with him from the king and queen of Spain addressed to

Columbus and his men captured natives to be used as slaves.

Vasco da Gama. Da Gama, a Portuguese explorer, had recently become the first European to pioneer a sea route to Asia around Africa. The letter read, "If you should meet at sea, you should treat each other in a friendly way, as befits captains and subjects of kings bound together by such kinship, love, and affection."

Fernando Columbus, son of Christopher Columbus and Beatrice Enriquez de Harana

Columbus's fourth expedition was his final one, and it proved to be even more disastrous than his third had been. When Columbus arrived in Hispaniola in late June of 1502, the Spanish colonists would not allow him to come ashore. They were following the direct orders of Ferdinand and Isabella, who had warned the explorer to stay away from the colony.

Columbus wrote about his feelings of anger and hurt when he was turned away from Hispaniola:

> *What man has not been born ... who would not have died of despair when in such a storm he should be forbidden to*

land for his own safety and that of his little son, and brother, and shipmates, land that, by God's will, I had sweated blood for, to acquire for Spain?

With no choice but to sail on, Columbus and his crew became the first Europeans to visit Central America. In Panama, Columbus's men discovered some gold and set up a small settlement. Natives told Columbus that more gold was to be had nearby. In a letter to the king and queen, he wrote, "I learned … a man might collect in ten days as much gold as a child could carry, whenever he wished."

Columbus and his men soon angered the native people in Panama. Before long, Columbus and his crew were driven off the land and forced onto their ships. Before leaving, however, Columbus and his men took a number of native slaves along with them.

In need of supplies, Columbus and his men headed back to Hispaniola. Along the way, two of the vessels sank. The other two were battered and leaking. Columbus later wrote that, as a result of shipworms, the ships had "more holes than a honeycomb." In June 1503, Columbus beached

A shipworm is not a worm but rather a very long clam. Its two shells function as a tool for boring into the wood on which it feeds. The common shipworm of the North Atlantic Ocean may grow to 2 feet (60 centimeters) long, although its shells remain only 1/2 inch (12 millimeters) long.

the damaged ships on the coast of Jamaica.

Columbus and his remaining crew now found themselves stranded. They had few supplies and no way to send a message for help to Hispaniola. First, Columbus tried to send a note to the Spanish colony with some natives. Then, a crew member named Diego Méndez tried to reach Santo Domingo in a canoe. On his first try, Méndez was imprisoned by island natives for a time before escaping. Despite the dangers, Méndez was determined to reach Hispaniola. He later wrote about his rescue mission:

> *I navigated for five days and four nights without leaving hold of the oar, steering the canoe while my companions rowed ... at the end of five days, I should reach the island of Española ... there having been two days during which we had neither eaten nor drunk. ... I beached my canoe ... there I remained two days resting. ... I left my canoe and made my way by land to Xaragua, where I found the governor. ... He detained me for seven months. ... I went on foot to the district of Santo Domingo, and I remained there expecting ships to come from [Spain] ... three ships [came] I bought one ... and sent her to where the admiral was ... I myself went forward in the other two ships to give an account to the king and queen of all that had occurred on that voyage.*

Méndez was proud of his rescue mission. In his will, he asked his family to place "a great stone, the best that they can find" over his tomb. On the stone, he asked that they carve a picture of a canoe.

During his four voyages, Columbus wrote many letters to Spanish rulers and officials.

While Columbus and his men waited to be rescued, the explorer became ill, possibly with gout. Gout is a painful disease that causes the joints to swell. While he was sick, nearly half his men rebelled, leaving his group to set up their own camp. Columbus's brother, Bartholomew, later brought the men under control.

The natives of Jamaica caused problems for the stranded men as well. To convince them that he was all-powerful, Columbus accurately predicted a total lunar eclipse using a star chart. The trick worked, and the natives didn't bother the marooned men for the rest of their stay.

While stranded on Jamaica, Columbus thought about his former glory and compared it to his current situation. He wrote to King Ferdinand and Queen Isabella,

Columbus accurately predicted an eclipse to convince the natives of his power.

> *I came to serve at the age of twenty-eight years, and now I have not a hair on my body that is not grey, and my body is*

infirm, and whatever remained to me from those years of service has been spent and taken away from me and sold, and from my brothers, down to my very coat, without my being heard or seen, to my great dishonour. It must be believed that this was not done by your royal command. The restitution of my honour, the reparation of my losses, and the punishment of him who did this, will spread abroad the fame of your nobility. ... I pray your Highnesses to pardon me. I am so ruined as I have said; hitherto I have wept for others; now, Heaven have mercy upon me, and may the earth weep for me. ... Weep for me, whoever has charity, truth, and justice.

Columbus's stay in Jamaica was miserable. In another letter to the king and queen, he wrote, "I beg Your Highnesses that if I have said anything against Your Royal wishes that I be pardoned; I am in such anguish and to such an extreme, that it is a marvel that I am alive and not going crazy. ... I also beg Your Highnesses, if it please God, to take me out of here."

On June 28, 1504, Columbus and his men were finally rescued. They had spent more than a year marooned on Jamaica. The explorer was allowed to enter Santo Domingo on Hispaniola, and he stayed there for a while before sailing for Spain.

Columbus left the New World behind for the final time on September 12, 1504. After landing in Spain in early November, he and his son Fernando settled in Seville. There, Columbus waited for the king and queen to summon him to court. Less than three weeks after his arrival, however, Queen Isabella died, and Columbus lost his strongest friend and ally at court.

Although he was only in his mid-50s, Columbus's health was rapidly declining. The explorer suffered constantly from arthritis, an illness that causes swelling and pain in the body's joints. His eyesight was also failing him.

Columbus suffered from poor health for much of his final years of life.

Columbus still believed that he had discovered a

new route to Asia, and he spent the final years of his life writing letters to various officials in Spain and Italy in the hope that someone would restore to him the honor, power, and glory he had enjoyed after his first voyage. He even requested help from the pope.

By the end of his life, however, Columbus seemed resigned to the fact that he would never recover what he had once had. In a letter to a friend, he wrote,

> *And it seems that His Highness [Ferdinand] does not intend to comply with what he has promised together with the Queen ... by word and writing. I believe that for me to struggle to the contrary ... would be to whip the wind; and it would be well that I now let God our Master do [it], since I have done what I could.*

The last line of the letter is consistent with Columbus's actions at other times in his life. On many occasions, he reached a point at which he turned his fate over to God, realizing that it was beyond his own control. Whether he was enduring a terrible storm, sitting in chains after his arrest, waiting for approval from kings and queens, or making the decision to cross the Atlantic in the first place, Columbus looked to the heavens for help. Now, in his final days, he would need it more than ever.

A
CRISTOFORO COLOMBO
PER LA PATRIA

Chapter

10 The Man Becomes a Myth

❧

Columbus died in Valladolid, Spain, in May 1506. He was 55 years old. Columbus had been following the Spanish court, probably hoping that the king would have a change of heart and restore him to his former glory. Despite Columbus's efforts on behalf of Spain, no note of his death was made in court or other records.

In his will, Columbus asked his son Diego to take care of his companion Beatrice:

> And I order that Beatriz Enriquez, mother of Don Fernando my son, be entrusted to him [Diego], that she may live honestly, as a person to whom I am so indebted. ... And that this be done to relieve my conscience because this weighs heavily on my soul.

This monument to Christopher Columbus stands in his hometown of Genoa, Italy.

He directed his son to give Beatrice the annual prize he had won by claiming to be the first to sight land in the New World.

Mystery surrounds Columbus's burial place. Some historians believe he is buried in Seville, Spain. Others think that his remains might be in Santo Domingo. Today, the true location of his grave remains unknown.

Even the proud and sometimes arrogant Columbus might have been surprised at the fame that grew up around him after his death. As early as the mid-1500s, Columbus was being hailed as the "Father of the New World." Maps and charts were redrawn to include information learned from the explorer's discoveries.

One of the first to write about Columbus was his son Fernando. In his *Historie*, Fernando recorded facts but also invented stories about his father's life. The purpose of his book was to make his father famous. It was also to put forth an alternate and perhaps more flattering version to two biographies that had already been published.

Columbus's greatest contribution was the exchange of goods between Europe and the Americas that came about during and after his voyages. Horses, cattle, pigs, and other livestock were introduced to the Americas from Europe. Europeans brought sugarcane, wheat, rice, and coffee to the

HISTORIE
Del S. D. Fernando Colombo;

Nelle quali s'ha particolare, & vera relatione
della vita, & de' fatti dell'Ammiraglio
D. CHRISTOFORO COLOMBO,
suo padre:

Et dello scoprimento, ch'egli fece dell'INDIE
Occidentali, dette MONDO NVOVO,
hora possedute dal Sereniss.
Re Catolico:

Nuouamente di lingua Spagnuola tradotte nell'Italiana
dal S. Alfonso Vlloa.

CON PRIVILEGIO.

IN VENI   M D LXXI.
Appresso Francesi.   *Francesчи Sanese.*

Columbus's son Fernando wrote one of the first accounts of the voyages to the New World.

Americas as well. And from the New World to old Europe came corn, potatoes, tomatoes, tobacco, peanuts, beans, peppers, and squash.

One important exchange was the horse. Left behind in the Americas after Spanish conquistadors returned to Europe, the horse completely changed the lifestyle of the region's native peoples. The natives soon began using the horse to hunt and raid neighboring villages.

Not all the exchanges were positive. The Spanish also brought diseases that wiped out thousands of native people. The native people had no natural resistance to these new diseases, which included smallpox, measles, chicken pox, typhus, and

The horse was not known in the Americas before the voyages of Columbus.

yellow fever. Smallpox was the deadliest. By the early 1600s, the native Taino people were extinct—and they weren't the only natives affected. Some experts estimate that European diseases killed about nine out of every 10 natives.

Smallpox is a disease that dates from the time of ancient Egypt or before. It has occurred around the world in epidemics throughout history, accounting for more deaths over time than any other infectious disease. Today, vaccination programs have eliminated smallpox worldwide.

People were in the Americas long before Columbus and his crew landed, and Viking explorers likely found the lands much earlier. Nevertheless, Christopher Columbus is remembered as the person who "discovered" America. Although he has been criticized for his treatment of the native peoples, he had vision and courage. His voyage into the unknown set an example for adventure and exploration and changed both Europe and America forever.

Columbus's successes led to other new discoveries. Encouraged by Columbus's triumphs, other explorers were able to get funding for their voyages and make their own discoveries. With each new voyage, new things were learned, making each successive crossing easier and more successful than those that came before. None of it could have happened had Columbus not gone first.

COLUMBUS'S LIFE

1479
Marries Felipa Moniz, a Portuguese noblewoman

1465
Goes to sea for the first time

1451
Born in Genoa, Italy

1450

1473
Astronomer Nicolaus Copernicus is born in Torún, Poland

1452
Leonardo da Vinci is born

WORLD EVENTS

1485

King John II of
Portugal refuses to
sponsor Columbus's
expedition; wife
Felipa dies

1488

Son Fernando is born
to Columbus and
companion Beatrice
Enriquez de Harana

1480

Son Diego is
born

1485

1485

Henry VII is crowned
king of England,
beginning the 117-
year reign of
England's Tudor
dynasty

COLUMBUS'S LIFE

1493

Returns to Spain where he receives a hero's welcome; sets sail on a second voyage in September

1492

Receives sponsorship of king and queen of Spain; embarks on first voyage, reaching the Bahamas on October 12

1495

1491

Ignatius Loyola, founder of the Jesuit order, is born in Spain

1493

Maximilian I begins reign as Holy Roman Emperor

WORLD EVENTS

1494

Founds Isabela, the
Spanish colonial capital
in the New World

1496

Returns to
Spain, leaving
his brothers
in charge of
Hispaniola

1498

Embarks on
a third voyage
to the New World

1497

Vasco da Gama
becomes the first
western European
to find a sea route
to India

COLUMBUS'S LIFE

1500

Is arrested for mis-
management and
sent back to Spain
in chains

1502

Embarks on fourth
and final voyage in
May; visits Central
America

1500

1502

Montezuma II
becomes ruler
of Mexico's
Aztec empire

WORLD EVENTS

1503

Stranded with crew
on the island of
Jamaica

1504

Rescued from
Jamaica after
spending a full
year on the island

1506

Dies on May 20 in
Valladolid, Spain

1505

1503

Italian artist
Leonardo da Vinci
begins painting
the *Mona Lisa*

1509

Henry, Prince of
Wales, at age 18,
becomes King
Henry VIII of
England

DATE OF BIRTH: Around 1451

PLACE OF BIRTH: Genoa, Italy

FATHER: Domenico Columbo

MOTHER: Susanna Fontanarossa

EDUCATION: None

SPOUSE: Felipa Moniz
(around 1455–1485)

DATE OF MARRIAGE: 1479

CHILDREN: Diego Colón
(1480–1526)
Fernando Colón
(with Beatrice Enriquez
de Harana)
(1488–1539)

DATE OF DEATH: May 20, 1506

PLACE OF BURIAL: Unknown; possibly Seville,
Spain, or Santo Domingo,
Dominican Republic

IN THE LIBRARY

Cothran, Helen, ed. *The Conquest of the New World.* San Diego: Greenhaven Press, 2002.

Lepore, Jill. *Encounters in the New World: A History in Documents.* New York: Oxford University Press, 2000.

Maestro, Betsy. *Exploration and Conquest: The Americas After Columbus: 1500–1620.* New York: Mulberry Books, 1997.

Sundel, Al. *Christopher Columbus and the Age of Exploration in World History.* Berkeley Heights, N.J.: Enslow Publishers, 2002.

Tucker, Mary. *Christopher Columbus: A Hands-On History Look at the Life and Adventures of Explorer Christopher Columbus.* Carthage, Ill.: Teaching and Learning Company, 2002.

Viola, Herman J. and Carolyn Margolis. *Seeds of Change: Five Hundred Years Since Columbus.* Washington: Smithsonian Institution Press, 1991.

LOOK FOR MORE SIGNATURE LIVES
BOOKS ABOUT THIS ERA:

Nicolaus Copernicus: *Father of Modern Astronomy*
ISBN 0-7565-1812-6

Elizabeth I: *Queen of Tudor England*
ISBN 0-7565-0988-2

Galileo: *Astronomer and Physicist*
ISBN 0-7565-0813-4

Johannes Gutenberg: *Inventor of the Printing Press*
ISBN 0-7565-0989-0

Michelangelo: *Sculptor and Painter*
ISBN 0-7565-0814-2

Francisco Pizarro: *Conqueror of the Incas*
ISBN 0-7565-0815-0

William Shakespeare: *Playwright and Poet*
ISBN 0-7565-0816-9

ON THE WEB

For more information on *Christopher Columbus*, use FactHound to track down Web sites related to this book.

1. Go to *www.facthound.com*
2. Type in a search word related to this book or this book ID: 0756508118
3. Click on the *Fetch It* button.

Your trusty FactHound will fetch the best Web sites for you!

HISTORIC SITES

The Mariners' Museum
100 Museum Drive
Newport News, VA 23606
757/596-2222
To see exhibits about navigators

Corpus Christi Museum of Science and History
1900 North Chaparral St.
Corpus Christi, TX 78401
361/883-2862
To see reproductions of Columbus's three ships, built by the Spanish to commemorate the 500th anniversary of Columbus's voyages to America

ambassador
a person who acts as a representative, often of his or her country

artisans
people who are skilled in a particular craft or crafts

colony
a group of people who leave their own country and settle in another land

conquistadors
Spanish conquerors of the 1500s who claimed lands in the Americas for Spain

cooper
a person who makes or repairs wooden barrels

courtier
a person who attends a royal court

flagship
the finest, largest, or most important ship in a fleet

mariner
a person who navigates and sails a ship

merchants
people whose business is buying goods and selling them for profit

monarchs
kings and queens

mutiny
an open rebellion against authority

navigation
the use of charts, maps, compasses, or the stars to plan the course of a trip

Chapter 2

Page 17, line 7: Miles H. Davidson. *Columbus Then and Now: A Life Reexamined.* Norman, Okla.: University of Oklahoma Press, 1997, p. 31.

Chapter 3

Page 32, line 8: Oliver Dunn and James E. Kelley, Jr., trans. *The Diario of Christopher Columbus's First Voyage to America, 1492–1493.* Norman, Okla.: University of Oklahoma Press, 1988, p. 261.

Chapter 4

Page 39, line 23: *Columbus Then and Now: A Life Reexamined,* p. 218.
Page 41, line 15: *The Diario of Christopher Columbus's First Voyage to America, 1492–1493,* p. 29.

Page 42, line 6: *Columbus Then and Now: A Life Reexamined,* p. 216.

Chapter 5

Page 45, line 3: Ibid., p. 223.

Page 45, line 15: Margarita Zamora. *Reading Columbus.* Berkeley, Calif.: University of California Press, p. 78.

Page 46, line 1: Ibid.

Page 47, line 3: Ibid., p. 192.

Page 48, line 8: *Columbus Then and Now: A Life Reexamined,* p. 273.

Page 48, line 24: *Reading Columbus,* p. 76.

Page 49, line 2: Cecil Jane, trans. *The Four Voyages of Columbus: A History in Eight Documents Including Five by Christopher Columbus.* New York: Dover Publications, Inc., 1988, p. 10.

Chapter 6

Page 55, line 3: *The Diario of Christopher Columbus's First Voyage to America, 1492–1493,* p. 305.

Page 56, sidebar: Ibid., p. 323.

Page 57, line 23: Ibid., p. 307.

Page 58, line 13: *Reading Columbus,* pp. 194–195.

Page 58, line 24: *Columbus Then and Now: A Life Reexamined,* p. 280.

Chapter 7

Page 63, line 15: Ibid., p. 316.

Page 64, line 9: Ibid., p. 317.

Page 65, line 7: Ibid., p. 325.

Page 66, line 10: *Reading Columbus,* p. 212.

Page 67, line 3: *Columbus Then and Now: A Life Reexamined,* p. 339.

Page 68, line 8: Ibid., p.382.

Page 68, line 20: Ibid.

Page 68, line 26: Ibid., p. 360.

Page 71, line 4: Ibid., p. 393.

Chapter 8

Page 74, sidebar: *The Four Voyages of Columbus: A History in Eight Documents Including Five by Christopher Columbus*, p. 30.

Page 77, line 27: Benjamin Keen, trans. *The Life of the Admiral Christopher Columbus by His Son Ferdinand.* New Brunswick, N.J.: Rutgers University Press, 1959, p. 223.

Chapter 9

Page 81, line 8: *Columbus Then and Now: A Life Reexamined*, p. 118.

Page 82, line 7: Hans Koenig. *Columbus: His Last Enterprise.* New York: Monthly Review Press, 1976, p. 109.

Page 82, line 25: Ibid., p. 110.

Page 83, line 10: *The Four Voyages of Columbus: A History in Eight Documents Including Five by Christopher Columbus*, p. 88.

Page 83, line 27: *Columbus Then and Now: A Life Reexamined*, p. 455.

Page 84, line 12: Ibid., p. 456.

Page 85, line 2. *The Four Voyages of Columbus: A History in Eight Documents Including Five by Christopher Columbus*, pp. 138–140.

Page 86, line 8: Ibid., pp. 138–140.

Page 87, sidebar: *Columbus Then and Now: A Life Reexamined*, p. 461.

Page 89, line 10: Ibid., 464.

Chapter 10

Page 91, line 10: *Columbus: His Last Enterprise*, p. 71.

Davidson, Miles H. *Columbus Then and Now: A Life Reexamined.* Norman, Okla.: University of Oklahoma Press, 1997.

Dunn, Oliver, and James E. Kelley, Jr., trans. *The Diario of Christopher Columbus's First Voyage to America, 1492–1493.* Norman, Okla.: University of Oklahoma Press, 1988.

Jane, Cecil, trans. *The Four Voyages of Columbus: A History in Eight Documents Including Five by Christopher Columbus.* New York: Dover Publications, Inc., 1988.

Keen, Benjamin, trans. *The Life of the Admiral Christopher Columbus by His Son Ferdinand.* New Brunswick, N.J.: Rutgers University Press, 1959.

Koenig, Hans. *Columbus: His Last Enterprise.* New York: Monthly Review Press, 1976.

Phillips, William D. Jr., and Carla Rahn Phillips. *The Worlds of Christopher Columbus.* New York: Cambridge University Press, 1992.

Zamora, Margarita. *Reading Columbus.* Berkeley, Calif.: University of California Press, 1993.

Robin S. Doak has been writing for children for more than 14 years. A former editor of *Weekly Reader* and *U*S*Kids* magazine, Ms. Doak has authored fun and educational materials for kids of all ages. Some of her work includes biographies of explorers such as Henry Hudson and John Smith, as well as other titles in this series. Ms. Doak is a past winner of the Educational Press Association of America Distinguished Achievement Award. She lives with her husband and three children in central Connecticut.

Image Credits

Library of Congress, cover (top), 4–5, 36, 38, 93, 98 (top left), 99 (bottom); Giraudon/Art Resource, N.Y., cover (bottom), 2, 59; Bettmann/Corbis, 8, 44; Scala/Art Resource, N.Y., 10, 16, 60, 72, 88, 96 (top), 100 (top), 101 (top); Hulton/Archive by Getty Images, 12, 49, 85, 98 (bottom), 100 (bottom); North Wind Picture Archives, 14, 18, 20, 33, 94; Stock Montage/Getty Images, 24, 43; Mary Evans Picture Library, 26, 27, 29, 34, 54, 62, 65, 69, 75, 76, 77, 78, 80, 82, 86, 97, 98 (top right), 99 (top); The Granger Collection, New York, 53; Bradley Smith/Corbis, 67; Corbis, 70; Vanni Archive/Corbis, 90; Courtesy History of Science Collections, University of Oklahoma Libraries, 96 (bottom); Wildside Press, 101 (bottom).